Date: 3/17/16

J 636.8 CON
Conley, Kate A.,
Kurilian bobtail cats /

Kurilian Bobtail Cats

Kate Conley

Checkerboard
Library
An Imprint of Abdo Publishing
abdopublishing.com

abdopublishing.com

Published by Abdo Publishing, a division of ABDO, PO Box 398166, Minneapolis, MN 55439.
Copyright © 2016 by Abdo Consulting Group, Inc. International copyrights reserved in all
countries. No part of this book may be reproduced in any form without written permission from
the publisher. Checkerboard Library™ is a trademark and logo of Abdo Publishing.

Printed in the United States of America, North Mankato, Minnesota.
042015
092015

THIS BOOK CONTAINS
RECYCLED MATERIALS

Cover Photo: Photo by Helmi Flick
Interior Photos: Alamy pp. 7, 19, 21; Photos by Helmi Flick pp. 5, 11, 13;
      iStockphoto pp. 1, 9, 15, 17

Series Coordinator: Tamara L. Britton
Editors: Tamara L. Britton, Bridget O'Brien
Art Direction: Neil Klinepier

Library of Congress Cataloging-in-Publication Data

Conley, Kate A., 1977- author.
  Kurilian bobtail cats / Kate Conley.
      pages cm. -- (Cats. Set 9)
  Includes index.
  ISBN 978-1-62403-812-9
1. Cats--Juvenile literature. 2. Cat breeds--Juvenile literature. I. Title.
  SF445.7.C655 2016
  636.8--dc23
                            2015006608

Contents

Lions, Tigers, and Cats 4

Kurilian Bobtail Cats. 6

Qualities 8

Coat and Color 10

Size 12

Care 14

Feeding. 16

Kittens. 18

Buying a Kitten. 20

Glossary 22

Websites 23

Index 24

Lions, Tigers, and Cats

While prowling along a riverbank, a cat suddenly reaches into the water. It grabs a salmon and pulls it from the water. This is a common catch for a wild Kurilian Bobtail. This **breed** has amazing hunting skills.

Like other cats, the Kurilian Bobtail is a member of the family **Felidae**. This family includes big cats that live in the wild, such as lions and tigers. It also includes small cats that live in homes as pets.

Members of this family share many **traits**. They are all hunters with sharp claws and pointed teeth. These animals are excellent climbers, jumpers, and stalkers. They move with purpose and grace.

The Kurilian Bobtail is a popular pet in Russia. It is rare elsewhere. However, the **breed** is sure to gain admirers as people learn about its sweet, gentle nature.

The Kurilian Bobtail cat

Kurilian Bobtail Cats

Kurilian Bobtails come from the Kuril Islands, a chain of islands between Russia and Japan. The cats have lived there for more than 200 years.

No one is certain how the cats came to live on the islands. Many people believe they arrived on fishing boats. These boats often had cats on board to control **rodents**. Some of the cats may have escaped when the boats docked there.

The Kuril Islands have a cold climate. To survive, Kurilian Bobtails became excellent hunters. They caught rabbits, snakes, squirrels, and mice. They could catch salmon that weighed up to ten pounds (4.5 kg). When hunting as a pack, Kurilian Bobtails could even catch small bears!

In the 1950s, scientists and soldiers brought a few Kurilians back to Russia. As the **breed** spread, it gained the attention of cat lovers in Europe. In 1996, the World Cat Federation recognized the Kurilian Bobtail. The International Cat Association did the same in 2012.

The Kurilian Bobtail is a natural breed. This means the cat developed on its own without human interference.

Qualities

Kurilian Bobtails are playful, social animals. These loyal cats love to be around their owners. Kurilian Bobtails are gentle, calm, and friendly. They make great pets for families with children, dogs, and other cats.

At home, Kurilians love to seek out the highest point they can find. They climb on top of bookcases, cabinets, and doorways. This is part of their hunting instincts. It allows them to observe a large area from one place.

Kurilian Bobtails are smart. Often, they only need to be shown something once before they understand what they are supposed to do. Kurilians are also a quiet **breed**. They make soft noises that sound like a bird chirping.

In general, Kurilian Bobtails are healthy cats. The **breed** developed by nature, not humans. So, these cats have fewer chances of health problems.

The Kurilian is an intelligent and curious breed. Expect this cat to investigate questionable objects!

Coat and Color

A Kurilian Bobtail's coat can be either short or long. In both cases, the coat is fine and **dense**. The fur feels soft and silky. It lies flat against the cat's body. **Mats** are rarely a problem in the Kurilian Bobtail's coat. And, this **breed sheds** minimally. So, these cats are easy to groom.

Kurilian Bobtails can come in a variety of colors. The breed does not have one specific color or pattern. They can be cream, black, red, orange, or silver. Silver Kurilian Bobtails are especially prized.

The patterns on Kurilian Bobtails also show great variety. Some of the cats in this breed are one solid color. The **tabby** pattern has stripes and spots. The tortoiseshell pattern is a mix of two colors, usually orange and black.

A Kurilian's coat can be any traditional color in solids or patterns.

Size

Kurilian Bobtails are powerful cats. They are medium to large in size. Adult males can weigh up to 15 pounds (7 kg). Adult females weigh between 8 and 11 pounds (4 and 5 kg).

Both males and females have sturdy bodies with broad chests. Their back legs are a little longer than their front legs, which gives the back a small arch. A Kurilian Bobtail's face has wide cheekbones and yellow or green eyes. The rectangular **muzzle** is wider than it is long. The Kurilian's **tufted** ears have rounded tips.

The Kurilian Bobtail's most distinctive feature is its tail. Most tails are between two and ten **vertebrae** long. The vertebrae bend and twist, giving the tails a variety of shapes. Some Kurilians have short tails that look like pom-poms. Others have longer tails shaped like hooks, spirals, or brushes.

Each Kurilian Bobtail's tail is as unique as a fingerprint. No two tails are alike.

Care

To feel safe and happy at home, Kurilian Bobtails need some special supplies. A cat needs food and water, toys, and a soft bed. A cat also needs a **litter box**. Waste needs to be cleaned from the litter box every day.

Giving a cat a scratching post is also important. In the wild, cats scratch on trees. This keeps their claws sharp. It also feels good! Providing a scratching post will stop a cat from scratching furniture, walls, and curtains.

To stay healthy, a cat must visit a veterinarian. The vet can give the cat a checkup. The vet can also give a cat its **vaccines**. If the cat needs to be **spayed** or **neutered**, the vet can do that, too.

A Kurilian will appreciate
a bed of its own.

Feeding

Cats need to eat quality cat food. Food gives a cat its energy, as well as providing all the **nutrients** needed to stay healthy. Cats also need fresh water. It should be available at all times. Treats are okay, but only once in a while!

Cats usually eat two times a day. The meals should be spaced out, so cats eat about every eight hours. The amount of food a cat receives depends on its activity level. Some cats like to lay in the sun all day. They need less food than a cat that plays all day.

Some cats can be picky about the food they eat. They often only like moist cat food, which is chewy and soft. It is much closer to what a cat would eat in the wild. Some cats don't mind dry food, which is crunchy and hard.

Keeping a cat's bowls clean will help it stay healthy.

Kittens

Most cats are able to mate at 7 to 12 months of age. After mating, a female Kurilian Bobtail is **pregnant** for about 65 days. There are usually two or three kittens in a **litter**.

When the kittens are born, they are helpless. They can't see or hear. The kittens develop their senses after 10 to 12 days. At three weeks, they can walk around and explore.

For the first five weeks, the kittens drink their mother's milk. Then, they are **weaned** onto solid food. This is also when they learn to use a **litter box**.

The kittens learn and grow every day. When they are 12 to 16 weeks old, they are old enough to leave their mother. Then they can be adopted into a loving, forever home.

Kurilian Bobtails produce just one litter a year.
So, the kittens are very rare.

Buying a Kitten

Adopting a kitten is exciting! Families adopt kittens from many different places. They can choose to go to a **breeder** or a shelter. Others adopt kittens from friends, families, or neighbors.

Have you decided a Kurilian Bobtail is the right cat for you? If so, look for a responsible breeder. These are rare cats, so you may have to wait for a kitten to become available.

Before you bring a kitten home, you will need basic supplies. So have a soft bed, a clean **litter box**, a scratching post, and some toys available. Kittens also need special food to provide them with the **nutrients** they need.

Most important, kittens need lots of love and attention. As your kitten grows into a cat, it will provide years of joy. A well cared for Kurilian Bobtail will be a loving family member for 15 to 20 years.

There are fewer than 100 of these special cats in the United States.

Glossary

breed - a group of animals sharing the same ancestors and appearance. A breeder is a person who raises animals. Raising animals is often called breeding them.

dense - thick or compact.

Felidae (FEHL-uh-dee) - the scientific Latin name for the cat family. Members of this family are called felids. They include lions, tigers, leopards, jaguars, cougars, wildcats, lynx, cheetahs, and domestic cats.

litter - all of the kittens born at one time to a mother cat.

litter box - a box filled with cat litter, which is similar to sand. Cats use litter boxes to bury their waste.

mat - a tangled mass.

muzzle - an animal's nose and jaws.

neuter (NOO-tuhr) - to remove a male animal's reproductive glands.

nutrient - a substance found in food and used in the body. It promotes growth, maintenance, and repair.

pregnant - having one or more babies growing within the body.

rodent - any of several related animals that have large front teeth for gnawing. Common rodents include mice, squirrels, and beavers.

shed - to cast off hair, feathers, skin, or other coverings or parts by a natural process.

spay - to remove a female animal's reproductive organs.

tabby - a coat pattern featuring stripes or splotches of a dark color on a lighter background. Individual hairs are banded with light and dark colors.

trait - a quality or feature of something.

tuft - a small bunch of feathered hair that grows close together.

vaccine (vak-SEEN) - a shot given to prevent illness or disease.

vertebra - one of the small bones that are linked together to form the backbone.

wean - to accustom an animal to eating food other than its mother's milk.

Websites

To learn more about Cats,
visit **booklinks.abdopublishing.com**. These links are routinely
monitored and updated to provide the most current information available.

Index

A

adoption 18, 20

B

body 10, 12
breeder 20

C

care 14, 16, 20
character 4, 5, 8
claws 14
coat 10
color 10, 12

E

ears 12
Europe 7
exercise 16
eyes 12

F

Felidae (family) 4
food 14, 16, 18, 20

G

grooming 10

H

health 9, 14, 16, 20
history 6, 7
hunting 4, 6

I

International Cat
    Association, The 7

J

Japan 6

K

kittens 18, 20
Kuril Islands 6

L

legs 12
life span 20
litter box 14, 18, 20

M

muzzle 12

N

neuter 14

R

reproduction 18
Russia 5, 6, 7

S

scratching post 14, 20
senses 18
shedding 10
size 12
spay 14

T

tail 12
teeth 4
toys 14, 20
treats 16

V

vaccines 14
veterinarian 14
voice 8

W

water 14, 16
World Cat Federation 7